Discovering the God We Call Father

A Catholic Bible Study on the Lord's Prayer

Published by The Word Among Us Press, 9639 Doctor Perry Road
Ijamsville, Maryland 21754
www.wordamongus.org
12 11 10 09 08 1 2 3 4 5
ISBN: 978-1-59325-136-9

Nihil Obstat: The Reverend Michael Morgan, Chancellor
Censor Librorum
April 28, 2008

Imprimatur: +Most Reverend Victor Galeone
Bishop of Saint Augustine
April 28, 2008

Cover design by David Crosson
Cover art: Ansiaux, Antoine (1764-1840)
Christ Blessing the Children (Suffer Little Children). 1820.
Photo credit: Réunion des Musées Nationaux/Art Resource, NY

Library of Congress Control Number: 2008925006

Discovering the God We Call Father

A Catholic Bible Study on the Lord's Prayer

Rich Cleveland

Table of Contents

Introduction

Why would a person choose to participate in a Bible study on the prayer that our Lord taught his disciples? I can think of several reasons: We may have a desire to have a deeper prayer life or a deeper communion with God. We may want a greater awareness that our prayer is being heard and accepted by the Father. We may want to take on the heart of Jesus by studying how he prayed and by asking for that same heart. Or we may want to discover in a deeper way just who our Father is and what we should ask of him.

For Catholics, the Our Father is a familiar family prayer that we can pray when we gather together. It's also a "fail-safe" prayer that we can fall back on in times of crisis and emotional turmoil, when we know not how or what to pray. It brings us deep consolation and stability in times of need.

St. Cyprian, a Church father, described the Our Father in this way:

> The Lord's Prayer contains many great mysteries of our faith. In these few words there is great spiritual strength, for this summary of divine teaching contains all of our prayers and petitions. And so, the Lord commands us: Pray then like this: Our Father, who art in heaven. (Cyprian, *Treatise on the Lord's Prayer* 4.9)

My hope for you, the reader, is that you will come to a more profound understanding of some of those "great mysteries of our faith" contained in this prayer and that each of its petitions will take on new meaning as you pray them. Most of all, I pray that you will develop a new consciousness of your relationship to the Father and will realize that *you* are his dearly beloved child, an heir with Christ to all that is the Father's.

One of the most important things you can do as you complete this study is to pray over each part of the lesson. If you simply read the material and fill in the blanks, you could complete the weekly lesson in approximately one hour. However, if you pause after reading each section of the study, reflect on the things that stand out to you, and talk about them with God in prayer, it could take you two hours or more—but it will be time well spent. The difference the additional hour will make will be as astounding as the difference between just reading the literature accompanying a bottle of medicine and actually taking the medicine. Healing and growth come about by *ingesting* the words of life that are Scripture, and prayerful meditation allows us to do that.

Practical Suggestions:

Here are some ways to enhance your experience of this Bible study:

• Begin your study early in the week so that you have adequate time to think and pray about what you are learning.

• Consider the words of Jeremiah 15:16, and pray that this might be your experience as you study:

Your words were found, and I ate them,
    and your words became to me a joy
    and the delight of my heart;
for I am called by your name,
    O Lord, God of hosts.

• Several sections require that you simply read and digest the concepts. The best way to do that is to mark the Scripture text as you read, making note of those phrases that stand out to you. This is often the way the Holy Spirit will bring a concept to your attention.

• Write out your answers to questions in well-developed paragraphs rather than with just two or three words. Remember, "Thoughts disentangle themselves when they pass through the lips and the fingertips."

• Prior to the weekly group meeting, review your lesson and choose six of the most meaningful things you have learned, so that when you have an opportunity to discuss the material, you will be focused. Also, write in the margin of your study those questions you want to discuss.

• Develop meaningful relationships with those in your discussion group by meeting for coffee or a meal. Ask one another questions such as "What has been most meaningful to you about the study we're doing?" or "Where are you in your journey with Christ these days?" You will find that your relationships will be enhanced as you share your life in Christ together.

• Finally, consider making the closing prayer of each session your daily prayer throughout each week of this study.

I am certain that the Lord will richly bless the efforts you put forth to study and share his word, and that he will answer the request that his disciples made of him: "Lord, teach us to pray" (Luke 11:1).

Rich Cleveland

Chapter 1

Discipleship Begins with Prayer

Luke 11:1-4

[1]He was praying in a certain place, and when he ceased, one of his disciples said to him, "Lord, teach us to pray, as John taught his disciples." [2]And he said to them, "When you pray, say:

"Father, hallowed be your name. Your kingdom come. [3]Give us each day our daily bread; [4]and forgive us our sins, for we ourselves forgive every one who is indebted to us; and lead us not into temptation."

In fifteen years of teaching Catholic small-group Bible studies and working with men's ministries, I have often asked fellow Catholics to either open or close a meeting with prayer. My request has been met many times with a response such as "Oh, I can't," or "Not me!" Invariably these individuals were actively involved in their parishes, and many also held leadership positions in their jobs, yet they felt intimidated about praying spontaneously and aloud. This shouldn't be case, although perhaps Jesus' disciples felt a similar sense of inadequacy.

In the early days of following Jesus, the apostles asked, "Lord, teach us to pray." Surely these men were devout Israelites who practiced the Hebrew faith and were familiar with its culture of prayer. But somehow their brief exposure to John the Baptist and their more intimate involvement with Jesus made them recognize that something was missing from their own relationship to the Father.

Especially as they witnessed Jesus in prayer, they sensed that there was a qualitative difference between his prayer and their own. They had followed Jesus long enough and had heard him explain what true worship of the Father involves often enough to realize that they were inadequate for the task. Undoubtedly they had also observed that first John the Baptist and then Jesus could not have carried out their missions without the strength they gained through a deep and intimate prayer relationship with the Father.

When they asked Jesus, then, to teach them how to pray, he did indeed show them. And one of the first principles of teaching is that the teacher demonstrates through his or her example and lifestyle what is being communicated verbally. After having invited these twelve men to follow him and become his disciples, Jesus often took them with him when he went apart to pray. The disciples' observation of Jesus' prayer relationship with the Father is probably what whetted their appetite and created a desire within them to know how to pray. And throughout Jesus' life and ministry, as we observe it in the gospel accounts, he made prayer a major focus of all he did and a key ingredient in the spiritual formation of his disciples.

Was Jesus successful in teaching his disciples how to pray? Yes, so much so that after Pentecost, his disciples launched a ministry rooted in prayer, resulting in a boldness to preach the gospel despite the personal danger and cost. The rulers who tried to squelch Jesus' followers concluded "that they had been with Jesus," because they had become like him (Acts 4:13).

We are going to learn about prayer in a general way in this chapter, before discussing the various parts of the Lord's Prayer in the later chapters. We will discover some of what Jesus taught about prayer and other helpful guidelines from Scripture.

However, I'd like you to keep two realities in mind as we learn about prayer. First, you learn to pray by praying. Therefore, you will only grow in your prayer relationship with the Father if you take the time to pray, to experiment with different forms of prayer, and to pray with others. Second, remember that however feeble your prayer may seem to you, the Father welcomes it, listens to it, and answers it. He wants you to grow in your ability to pray, so that your relationship with him can grow. Remember, too, that your prayer is no less worthy if you are not experienced at prayer.

What a shame it would be if after completing eight lessons on the Our Father, our prayer life was unaffected. Perhaps we should take to heart the advice of St. Anselm:

> Insignificant man, escape from your everyday business for a short while, hide for a moment from your restless thoughts. Break off from your cares and troubles and be less concerned about your tasks and labors. Make a little time for God and rest a while in him.

Enter into your mind's inner chamber. Shut out everything but God and whatever helps you to seek him; and when you have shut the door, look for him. Speak now to God and say with your whole heart: I seek your face; your face, Lord, I desire.

Lord, my God, teach my heart where and how to seek you, where and how to find you. (Anselm, *Proslogion* 1)

▶Learning from Scripture

1.   a. In your own words, how would you define prayer?

_____

_____

_____

_____

_____

_____

b. Why do you think prayer is important?

_____

_____

_____

_____

_____

_____

2. Jesus' instructions regarding prayer are given in the context of the Sermon on the Mount and are bracketed by teachings on almsgiving and fasting.

    a. What do almsgiving (Matthew 6:1-4), prayer (6:5-8), and fasting (6:16-18) have in common? List at least three things.

    _____

    _____

    _____

    _____

    _____

    _____

    b. What practical application(s) do you see from the passage on prayer (Matthew 6:5-8)?

    _____

    _____

    _____

    _____

    _____

    _____

    c. As Catholics, we say many prayers repetitively. How can we prevent these prayers from becoming just "empty phrases" (Matthew 6:7)?

    _____

    _____

    _____

    _____

    _____

    _____

d. How do you respond to the truth that God knows what we need before we ask for it (Matthew 6:8)?

_____

_____

_____

_____

_____

_____

e. Jesus says that the Father rewards us when we give, pray, and fast in secret. How helpful should the reward motivation be in your prayer life?

_____

_____

_____

_____

_____

3. We can learn from Jesus by looking at his prayer prior to his passion in John 17.
a. After reading through this prayer, write down what you have learned about prayer.

_____

_____

_____

_____

_____

b. Out of the twenty-six verses in this prayer, how many include a request? List the specific petitions Jesus makes.

_____

_____

_____

_____

_____

_____

c. If the majority of Jesus' prayer is not about asking for something, what is it about?

_____

_____

_____

_____

_____

_____

d. Identify one thing you learned from Jesus' prayer that you can use to enhance your prayer life.

_____

_____

_____

_____

_____

_____

▶Real-Life Lessons

Only a few weeks after my conversion, my friends invited me to the Wiesbaden, Germany, Air Force chapel to meet with a half-dozen other Christian men. The chapel was empty, so we knelt around the altar rail to pray for other men we knew. Having limited experience with organized religion, I knew very little about prayer, so when it was my turn to pray, being a good military man, I began, "Sir, . . ." I'm sure our heavenly Father smiled warmly, as we often do at a child's first attempts at prayer.

A slightly older Christian friend, Gene, who was helping to form me in the faith, was the one who really taught me how to pray. We met together weekly for a Bible study, and after one particular study, Gene said, "Let's pray." He then knelt down next to the couch and folded his hands in prayer, and I followed suit. Gene prayed for several minutes, which that first time seemed like several hours, and then paused for me to pray. Initially, I simply stumbled along, repeating some of the things I had heard him say. However, over the next few weeks, I discovered both the way and the freedom to pray from the heart by listening to Gene's prayers and by expressing my own thoughts to God, both when we prayed together and when I prayed alone.

There is perhaps no greater motivation to be serious about discipleship and spiritual formation than to pray with someone who genuinely loves God.

▶Learning from the Church

Prayer is the offering in spirit that has done away with the sacrifices of old. What good do I receive from the multiplicity of your sacrifices? asks God. I have had enough of burnt offerings of rams, and I do not want the fat of lambs and the blood of bulls and goats. Who has asked for these from your hands?

What God has asked for we learn from the Gospel. The hour will come, he says, when true worshipers will worship the Father in spirit and in truth. God is a spirit, and so he looks for worshipers who are like himself.

We are true worshipers and true priests. We pray in spirit, and so offer in spirit the sacrifice of prayer. Prayer is an offering that belongs to God and is acceptable to him: it is the offering he has asked for, the offering he planned as his own. . . .

Its [prayer's] only art is to call back the souls of the dead from the very journey into death, to give strength to the weak, to heal the sick, to exorcise the possessed, to open prison cells, to free the innocent from their chains. Prayer cleanses from sin, drives away temptations, stamps out persecutions, comforts the fainthearted, gives new strength to the courageous, brings travelers safely home, calms the waves, confounds robbers, feeds the poor, overrules the rich, lifts up the fallen, supports those who are falling, sustains those who stand firm. . . .

What more need be said on the duty of prayer? Even the Lord himself prayed. To him be honor and power for ever and ever. Amen.

—**Tertullian,** *On Prayer* 28–29

What one or two important truths did you learn from the above material?

_____

_____

_____

_____

_____

_____

_____

▶Closing Prayer Together

Pray the following prayer daily during the week prior to discussing this chapter; then close your discussion by praying it in unison:

Loving Savior, be pleased to show yourself to us who knock, so that in knowing you we may love only you, love you alone, desire you alone, contemplate only you day and night, and always think of you. Inspire in us the depth of love that is fitting for you to receive as God. So may your love pervade our whole being, possess us completely, and fill all our senses, that we may know no other love but love for you who are everlasting. May our love be so great that the many waters of sky, land and sea cannot extinguish it in us: many waters could not extinguish love [see Song of Solomon 8:7].

May this saying be fulfilled in us also, at least in part, by your gift, Jesus Christ, our Lord, to whom be glory for ever and ever. Amen.

—**St. Columban,** from an instruction (*De compunctione* 12.2–3)

▶Notes

Chapter 2

Understanding Our Father

Matthew 6:9-13

[9]Pray then like this:

Our Father who art in heaven,
Hallowed be thy name.
[10]Thy kingdom come.
Thy will be done,
    On earth as it is in heaven.
[11]Give us this day our daily bread;
[12]And forgive us our trespasses,
    As we forgive those who trespass against us;
[13]And lead us not into temptation,
    But deliver us from evil.

Our Father who art in heaven." How strange it must have seemed to the Jewish disciples to be taught to open their prayer with such a personal and intimate salutation! Jewish men and women had always been taught that God is so holy, so transcendent, so high and exalted, that to utter his name was disrespectful. They would not even call him by the name he had given them, YHWH; instead, as they read or spoke of him, they used the name "LORD" (see *Catechism of the Catholic Church*, 209). Perhaps it was this intimate relationship the apostles observed when Jesus prayed that prompted them to ask Jesus to teach them to pray, to give them permission to also address the Almighty in such an intimate way.

For many of us, it is equally strange to call God "Father," not because we have been told it is wrong to use that name, but because the word conjures up images that are nothing like our heavenly Father. For instance, by the time I was born, my father had become an alcoholic, manifesting the characteristics of sullenness, a suddenly erupting temper, and physical and verbal abuse. The occasional moments of sobriety the family experienced, when he was pleasant and enjoyable to be around, were always shattered by an abrupt change back to his drunken state, which dashed our hopes and disappointed us bitterly.

Many other people are raised without any father figure in their lives or, in some cases, with only a part-time father who is often physically or emotionally unavailable. Still others only experience their father's love when they "measure up" and meet an elusive list of expectations. For better or for worse, our view of God is at least initially influenced by our earthly father, even if that father's character traits stand in sharp contrast to God's. Consequently, many find it strange and difficult to view God as Father and to address him in that way. To some extent, all of us need help redefining what it means that God is our Father.

We can better understand the fatherhood of God when we realize that when we were baptized into Christ, we became God's adopted sons and daughters. God is our Father, and Christ is our brother. This is what St. John speaks of in the first few paragraphs of his account of Jesus' life: "To all who received him, who believed in his name, he gave power to become children of God; who were born, not of blood nor of the will of the flesh nor of the will of man, but of God" (John 1:12-13). "For all who are led by the Spirit of God are sons of God. . . . and if children, then heirs, heirs of God and fellow heirs with Christ" (Romans 8:14, 17). According to these verses, then, we are God's children by an act of *his* will.

So far, we have reflected on the personal nature of God as our Father, but this phrase also introduces another important concept: the "our" in the Our Father includes all the members of Christ's body, as well as Christ himself. We are not an only child; we are members of a family. When we properly pray the Our Father, we are also praying the Father's blessing and will for all those other family members, both present and absent, here on earth and in heaven. And when people from all around the world pray the Our Father, we are also included in their prayers.

What a wonderful heritage! Regardless of the earthly father we had or the family into which we were born, through faith in Christ we can experience God as *our* Father, and with every waking moment, both in joy and in need, we can cry, "Abba, Father" (Mark 14:36). We will find a heavenly Father who is all powerful, ever present, all wise, and most important, all loving. And when we are too broken to pray, our holy family all around the world—including our mother, Mary—is praying for us.

As children adopted into God's family, we should turn to Jesus, who has always been with the Father, asking him to teach us what the Father is like and how to relate to him. After all, this is what he came to earth to do—to reveal the Father to us and to welcome us into his Father's family.

▶Learning from Scripture

1. Abraham was asked to sacrifice his and Sarah's only son, a son given to them in their old age. Read the account in Genesis 22:1-18, where Abraham is both a real, human father and a type of our heavenly Father. What is revealed about God's character in this incident?

_____

_____

_____

_____

_____

2. Jesus' parable of the prodigal son (or sons) gives us wonderful insights into the Father's love. Read Luke 15:11-32, and answer the following questions:

   a. Of the things the younger son said about his relationship with his father, what was true and what was not true?

_____

_____

_____

_____

_____

   b. What was true and what was not true about what the older son believed about his relationship with his father?

_____

_____

_____

_____

_____

_____

_____

c. What do you think the father wanted his sons to know about their relationships with him?

_____

_____

_____

_____

_____

_____

d. How does this parable help you in understanding your relationship with your heavenly Father?

_____

_____

_____

_____

_____

_____

3. Read Luke 12:29-32. What does it mean to seek the Father's kingdom, and what are the advantages of doing so?

_____

_____

_____

_____

_____

_____

_____

4.   Sacred Scripture teaches that God gives good gifts to those who ask (Matthew 7:7-11). Read 2 Corinthians 1:3-4 and Ephesians 1:17-20, and write a prayer asking God for one of the gifts he wants to give you that is listed in those passages.

_____

_____

_____

_____

_____

_____

▶Real-Life Lessons

For Jenny, thinking of God as Father had always been a struggle:

> King? Sure. Ruler? Of course. But Father? My knee-jerk reaction to thinking of God as Father used to be wince as I recalled images from my childhood of my own father: distant, angry, volatile, unfair, and moody. I spent years feeling like nothing I ever did or ever could do would really please my dad and make him love me. I eventually gave up on being loved just for me; instead I would strive for any acknowledgment or pat on the head I could get. Usually those "pats" came from things I achieved—good grades in school, music, sports, and so forth—not from who I was.
>
> Spiritually, I mirrored this behavior in my relationship with God. I tried to earn his love—and not earn his wrath. I thought that if I could just perform well enough, I would deserve his

love and approval. In the same fashion, feeling essentially unlovable, I tried to *do* things that might catch God's eye, making me more noticeable to him. I mastered being a busy "Martha," not a "Mary" who spent her time at Christ's feet, just being herself, being loved.

I now see myself through God's eyes as a daughter of the Most High and not merely the daughter of a man on earth. Now when I think of God as Father, I am thankful that my place in his family is secure. The longer I know him, the more I see that his track record with me is the most constant I have ever known. The more I trust him, the easier it is to let my earthly dad off the hook from all my unmet expectations. Also, as I seek to continually forgive my earthly dad for his inability to love me the way I needed (and need), I feel less compelled to earn God's favor. Instead I just sit, like Mary, confident and peaceful at my heavenly Father's feet.

▶Learning from the Church

"Our" Father refers to God. The adjective, as used by us, does not express possession, but an entirely new relationship with God.

When we say "our" Father, we recognize first that all his promises of love announced by the prophets are fulfilled in the *new and eternal covenant* in his Christ: we have become "his" people and he is henceforth "our" God. . . . Grammatically, "our" qualifies a reality common to more than one person. There is only one God, and he is recognized as Father by those who, through faith in his only Son, are reborn of him by water and the Spirit. The *Church* is this new communion of God and men. United with the only Son, who has become "the firstborn among many brethren," she is in communion with one and the same Father in one and the same Holy Spirit. . . .

For this reason, in spite of the divisions among Christians, this prayer to "our" Father remains our common patrimony and an urgent summons for all the baptized. In communion by faith in Christ and by Baptism, they ought to join in Jesus' prayer for the unity of his disciples.

Finally, if we pray the Our Father sincerely, we leave individualism behind, because the love that we receive frees us from it. The "our" at the beginning of the Lord's Prayer, like the "us" of the last four petitions, excludes no one. If we are to say it truthfully, our divisions and oppositions have to be overcome.
—*Catechism of the Catholic Church,* 2786–2787, 2790–2792

What one important truth did you learn from the above material?

_____

_____

_____

_____

_____

_____

_____

▶Closing Prayer Together

Pray the following prayer daily during the week prior to discussing this chapter; then close your discussion by praying it in unison:

Father, Abba, we lift our hearts to you in love, for in love you made us and called us into your love.

We do not know how to return your love in ways that are not wrapped up in self-love, but we nevertheless give you what we have—ourselves.

You are worthy of all of our trust, yet at times we have not trusted you; at times we have resented you and shoved you aside.

Thank you for remaining faithful to us, even when we were

unfaithful. We say, "Thank you!" Thank you for the many good things with which you have blessed us.

We pray, Abba, Father, that you will open our eyes to see your goodness and open our hearts and mouths to express our gratitude. Amen.

▶Notes

▶Notes

Chapter 3

Honoring Our Father

Matthew 6:9-13

[9]Pray then like this:
Our Father who art in heaven,
Hallowed be thy name.
[10]Thy kingdom come,
Thy will be done,
 On earth as it is in heaven.
[11]Give us this day our daily bread;
[12]And forgive us our trespasses,
 As we forgive those who trespass against us;
[13]And lead us not into temptation,
 But deliver us from evil.

The prayer Jesus taught his disciples has some six or seven petitions included within it, depending on how the text is divided. "Hallowed be thy name" is the first petition we encounter. To "hallow" something means to consider it holy, consecrated, and revered or set apart as sacred. Clearly our Lord Jesus is concerned that his Father's name be held in utmost esteem by people. This first petition is not unlike the second of the Ten Commandments: "You shall not take the name of the LORD your God in vain; for the LORD will not hold him guiltless who takes his name in vain" (Exodus 20:7).

What we do with God's name is a choice we make that when rightly made will bring us God's blessings. This is an important concept to grasp. The Father didn't give us commandments in order to make us miserable but so that we might maximize the good that comes from a proper relationship with him. Consequently, the extent to which we revere God and his name reveals much about the reality of God in our life.

Whenever we hallow, revere, and praise God's holy name, we hold him in the forefront of our minds. We also hold up his words, his character, and his dealings with us. In this way, he becomes a real presence in our lives, not simply some obscure concept that was taught to us when we were children.

This reality of God has a profound effect on our spirit, giving us an optimistic outlook and hope for the future. We see this effect at work in many passages in the Old Testament and especially in several psalms that summarize the history of Israel, such as Psalms 78 and 107. When the people of Israel forgot God and failed to hallow his name, they drifted from him, fell into sin and idolatry, and eventually became enslaved. Conversely, when they remembered God and rendered to him the honor and glory that was due him, their spirits were lifted and God set them free. Our ability to live a life of hope is dependent on our knowing intimately and consciously the God of hope; hallowing and praising God's name are crucial to that process of coming to know him. Theologian Romano Guardini reinforced this concept in his book *The Art of Praying*:

> It is "meet and just" to do homage to Him who is supreme greatness and glory; at the same time this act of homage is an act of self-realization for him who performs it. Man's real world is, as it were, above him. Praising God means ascending into that homeland of our spirit where, it may be said, we truly live. Thus we should practice giving praise to God. This discipline widens and edifies the spirit. (pp. 59–60)

What we do with God's name is a choice we make that affects both our spirit and our life. Unfortunately, we live in a society that has become so secularized that almost any crude or sacrilegious term is readily accepted as a legitimate expression, even within polite society. We hear these terms so often that we risk becoming numb to their effect and may even allow them to creep into our own vocabulary.

Imagine for a moment that some important dignitary, head of state, or Church official came to spend several hours or days with you. How would your language and deportment be affected? How much more, then, should you go out of your way to honor by word and action the name and person who is ever with us—our heavenly Father?

God's name is holy and worthy of awe, respect, obedience, and reverence. As mentioned previously, our Jewish forefathers held God's name in such reverence that they would not speak it aloud. Through Christ, the names of the Father, Son, and Holy Spirit have become as familiar as family names, and we have the freedom to use them in conversation—but not in derision, as a joke or curse, or for personal and manipulative purposes. We must once again recapture the holy importance the Father gives his name, and we can best do that by looking to sacred Scripture and the teachings of his Son.

▶Learning from Scripture

1. Write all the names for God you can recall from memory.

   _____

   _____

   _____

   _____

   _____

   _____

2. Read Exodus 3:13-14. What was the name God told Moses to use when Moses encountered him on Mount Sinai? Why do you think God referred to himself in this way?

   _____

   _____

   _____

   _____

   _____

   _____

3. In the Old Testament, God's name is often coupled with other words to remind the Israelites what the Father is like.
   a. In these eleven passages, how does God, or how do his people Israel, describe what he is like or what he does?
   Yahweh Elohim (Genesis 1:1; Isaiah 45:18)
   Yahweh-Yireh (Genesis 22:14)
   Yahweh-Rophe (Exodus 15:22-26)
   Yahweh-Nissi (Exodus 17:15)
   Yahweh-Maccaddeshcem (Exodus 31:13)

Yahweh-M'Kaddesh (Leviticus 20:8)
Yahweh-Shalom (Judges 6:24)
Yahweh-Rohi (Psalm 23:1)
Yahweh-Sabaoth (Isaiah 1:24)
Yahweh-Tsidkenu (Jeremiah 23:5-6)
Yahweh-Shammah (Ezekiel 48:35)

_____

_____

_____

_____

_____

_____

b. Which of the above names for God reflects your experience
with God? Why?

_____

_____

_____

_____

_____

_____

c. Of the names above, which one describes the way you would
especially like to experience God this year?

_____

_____

_____

_____

_____

4.   Read Luke 1:30-33 and Matthew 1:20-23.
     a. What does the name Jesus mean?

     _____

     _____

     _____

     _____

     _____

     _____

     b. How did Jesus' life on earth show us what the Father is like?

     _____

     _____

     _____

     _____

     _____

5.   After hearing Elizabeth's greeting, the Blessed Virgin Mary
     prayed the *Magnificat* (Luke 1:46-56). In what ways does her
     prayer hallow God's name?

     _____

     _____

     _____

     _____

     _____

6. What are some positive ways you can revere, or make hallowed, God's name?

_____

_____

_____

_____

_____

_____

▶Real-Life Lessons

Years ago there was a popular gospel song called "There's Just Something about That Name," and Al's experience has verified that truth—regarding both the name of Jesus and the name of our heavenly Father.

As a young man in the late 1960s, Al worked as a shipfitter's assistant in the Jacksonville, Florida, shipyards. Although Al had served in the military and had lived in an all-male dorm during college, he was surprised at the crudeness, vulgarity, and abuse of God's name that he encountered at his job. Al didn't enter into this kind of talk, and people noticed. In one-to-one conversations and in groups of only two or three men, fellow shipyard workers asked him why. In response to these inquiries, he was able to talk about his faith.

Although Al never said anything directly about their language or profane use of God's name, in a very short time God's name dropped out of their conversations with him, though the men's crudeness and vulgarity remained. When someone slipped up and used God's name in vain, that person would immediately say to Al, "Oh, excuse my French," or make some other attempt to apologize.

Like Al, I have also seen this reaction, both in the military and at other times. People inherently know that using God's name in vain is wrong, and in the face of a friend who professes belief in that name, they are embarrassed to continue using it, although they are not embarrassed to still be crude and vulgar. As Al discovered, there *is* something about God's name, and that something is that it should be hallowed.

▶Learning from the Church

> What therefore is the meaning of "hallowed be your name"? . . .
> When it is our settled conviction and belief that he who by
> nature is God over all is Holy of the Holies, we confess his
> glory and supreme majesty. We then receive his fear into our
> mind and lead upright and blameless lives. By this we become
> holy ourselves, and we may be able to be near unto the holy
> God. . . . The prayer is, therefore, "May your name be kept
> holy in us, in our minds and wills." This is the significance
> of the word *hallowed.* If a person says, "Our Father, hallowed
> be your name," he is not requesting any addition to be made
> to God's holiness. He rather asks that he may possess such a
> mind and faith to feel that his name is honorable and holy.
> The act is the source of life and the cause of every blessing.
> How must being this influenced by God be worthy of the
> highest estimation and useful for the salvation of the soul?
> —**Cyril of Alexandria,** Homily 72

What one important truth did you learn from the above material?

_____

_____

_____

_____

_____

_____

▶Closing Prayer Together

Pray the following prayer daily during the week prior to discussing this chapter; then close your discussion by praying it in unison:

You are God: we praise you;
You are the Lord: we acclaim you;
You are the eternal Father:
All creation worships you.

To you all angels, all the powers of heaven,
Cherubim and Seraphim, sing in endless praise:
Holy, holy, holy Lord, God of power and might,
heaven and earth are full of your glory.

The glorious company of apostles praise you.
The noble fellowship of prophets praise you.
The white-robed army of martyrs praise you.

Throughout the world the holy Church acclaims you:
Father, of majesty unbounded.
— *Te Deum*

▶Notes

▶Notes

Chapter 4

Living as Citizens of the Kingdom

Matthew 6:9-13

[9]Pray then like this:
Our Father who art in heaven,
Hallowed be thy name.
[10]Thy kingdom come,
Thy will be done,
    On earth as it is in heaven.
[11]Give us this day our daily bread;
[12]And forgive us our trespasses,
    As we forgive those who trespass against us;
[13]And lead us not into temptation,
    But deliver us from evil.

In its early years, the nation of Israel existed without a king. After the death of Moses, Joshua led the people into the land of Canaan. Then God raised up other leaders, called judges, who delivered the Israelites from danger by leading them into military battles. The Book of Judges reflects a national consciousness of being kingless: "In those days there was no king in Israel; every man did what was right in his own eyes" (21:25).

Later, however, the people demanded a king: "Behold, . . . appoint for us a king to govern us like all the nations" (1 Samuel 8:5). And although they clamored for an earthly king, the Israelites' subsequent behavior reflected a human characteristic—our innate dislike for being ruled.

Today the concept of kingdom rule seldom enters our consciousness. Of course, prior to the nineteenth century, this was not so, for the majority of the world's major political powers were ruled by monarchies and tried to expand their kingdoms by conquest. When territorial expansion was successful, the people in those conquered countries became subjects of the conquering kingdom, regardless of whether they spoke the language or had a similar culture—the conquered people became members of the kingdom by compulsion.

This was true of the Jews during the time Jesus lived on earth. The Israelites were a conquered people under Roman rule. They were undoubtedly very conscious of the rise and fall of political or national kingdoms and can be excused for not immediately grasping what Jesus meant when he spoke of the kingdom of God, or the kingdom of heaven.

However, the kingdom about which Jesus spoke is unique in many ways, not the least of which is that it compels no one to become a subject by force. The kingdom of God comes only through the welcoming response of its subjects to God's invitation and with God's ready help. The late Pope John Paul II explained it this way:

Salvation consists in believing and accepting the mystery of the Father and of his love, made manifest and freely given in Jesus through the Spirit. In this way the kingdom of God comes to be fulfilled: the kingdom prepared for in the Old Testament, brought about by Christ and in Christ, and proclaimed to all peoples by the Church. . . . (Pope John Paul II, *Mission of the Redeemer*, 12)

A second unique quality about the kingdom of God is that it is *not* a politically organized community and has no defined boundaries. Nevertheless, it does have a monarchical form of government, a king who holds a preeminent position. Because the kingdom of God is not political, does not have defined boundaries, and does not have a king who is visible to our eyes, it is often ignored—even by those who have chosen to become its subjects. In a unique way, the kingdom and the King are synonymous, as Pope John Paul II pointed out:

The kingdom of God is not a concept, a doctrine, or a program subject to free interpretation, but it is before all else a person with the face and name of Jesus of Nazareth, the image of the invisible God. If the kingdom is separated from Jesus, it is no longer the kingdom of God which he revealed. (Pope John Paul II, *Mission of the Redeemer*, 18)

The kingdom of God is in fact the reign of Jesus, King and Lord.

There is a story about a nineteenth-century boy who with all of his heart desired to leave home and go to the New World, the land of opportunity. He saved and saved until he had enough money to book passage on a ship. Coming on board, he brought his meager belongings and a small amount of food. During the days, the trip was fairly tolerable, but it was a different story at night, as he stood outside on the deck and looked through the window into the dining area, where people were warm, enjoying life, and feasting. Somewhat enviously, he would consume some of his diminishing food, curl up inside or under one of the lifeboats, and spend the night shivering.

Toward the end of the trip, he was discovered by one of the ship's stewards, who at first thought he was a stowaway. When the boy produced his ticket, the steward was astonished and asked, "Why are you living like this? Don't you know that with your ticket comes a warm room and three meals a day?" The boy was chagrined to realize that he had missed out on all the rights and privileges that should have been his on the ocean journey.

Many of us are like the boy on the ocean liner. Although we have been baptized into Christ, we choose to live as spiritual paupers, when in fact we could be enjoying the warmth, nourishment, and security that come with the "ticket" that Christ bought for us with his death and resurrection.

As we pray, "Thy kingdom come," may we be reminded of the many privileges that come from being subjects in the kingdom of God. Our King is a merciful king, our King is a gracious king, our King is a powerful king, and our King is a king who provides; his reign in our lives brings wonderful benefits. We could go on and on discovering and listing the wonderful attributes of our King and his kingdom, but we have the rest of our lives to do that. In this chapter, we mainly want to think more deeply about the King and the kingdom that we pray so often will "come."

▶Learning from Scripture

1. How does Acts 2:22-36 connect the Old Testament's promise of
    an eternal king and an everlasting kingdom with Jesus?

    _____

    _____

    _____

    _____

    _____

    _____

2. Review the following verses: Acts 2:37-38; Matthew 18:3-5;
    John 3:3-5. How does one gain entrance into the kingdom of
    God?

    _____

    _____

    _____

    _____

    _____

    _____

3. When we are citizens of the kingdom of God, we often look at
    life differently and respond in a way that is contrary to "worldly"
    wisdom. What revolutionary concepts are included in the fol-
    lowing verses:
    a. Matthew 5:3-10

    _____

    _____

    _____

    _____

    _____

_____

_____

_____

b. Matthew 20:1-16

_____

_____

_____

_____

_____

_____

4. Read the parable in Luke 14:15-24. What is one reason people fail to welcome the kingdom of God?

_____

_____

_____

_____

_____

5. Read Matthew 13:44-45. How should we respond to the kingdom of God?

_____

_____

_____

_____

_____

6. One of the privileges of kingdom living is that the King invites us to share in his mission. Read Luke 4:42-43; 8:1. How does Jesus describe his mission?

_____

_____

_____

_____

_____

_____

7. How does the Church serve the kingdom of God according to the following passages:
a. Matthew 16:15-19

_____

_____

_____

_____

_____

_____

b. Luke 9:1-2; 10:1-9

_____

_____

_____

_____

_____

8. How has your understanding changed regarding the kingdom of God and your desire that his "kingdom come"?

_____

_____

_____

_____

_____

_____

▶Real-Life Lessons

Millie, a young woman in her first year of college, came from a comfortable home, attended church fairly regularly, and was reasonably happy. When her sister invited her to join a small-group Bible study, she willingly came along, but she was somewhat turned off when the leader talked with her about something so personal as her relationship with Jesus. However, she agreed to continue with the Bible study as long as no one engaged her in that kind of conversation again.

But the time she invested reading Scripture and preparing the Bible study lessons soon began to have a positive effect. She started to realize that her life lacked the more intimate relationship with Christ that was promised in Scripture. She recognized that she was living primarily for herself but that Jesus desired to be her Lord. In her words, "One day when I was driving home from my Bible study, I realized that I needed to let Christ become the Lord of my life. So as I was driving, I simply talked to Jesus and told him I wanted to become his follower."

Millie's life changed right then and there. No, she didn't hear bells or whistles, but from that point forward, she made Christ the focus of her life. She resolved to know him better and to do his will as best she could. What Millie experienced is what Pope Benedict XVI wrote regarding the kingdom: "To pray for the Kingdom of God is to say to

Jesus: Let us be yours, Lord! Pervade us, live in us. . ." (*Jesus of Nazareth*, p. 147). That day Millie began experiencing what it means to live as a citizen in God's kingdom.

▶Learning from the Church

The Church is effectively and concretely at the service of the kingdom. This is seen especially in her preaching, which is a call to conversion. Preaching constitutes the Church's first and fundamental way of serving the coming of the kingdom in individuals and in human society. . . .

The Church . . . serves the kingdom by establishing communities and founding new particular churches, and by guiding them to mature faith and charity in openness toward others. . . .

The Church serves the kingdom by spreading throughout the world the "gospel values" which are an expression of the kingdom and which help people to accept God's plan. . . .

Finally, the Church serves the kingdom by her intercession, since the kingdom by its very nature is God's gift and work, as we are reminded by the gospel parables and by the prayer which Jesus taught us. We must ask for the kingdom, welcome it and make it grow within us; but we must also work together so that it will be welcomed and will grow among all people, until the time when Christ "delivers the kingdom to God the Father" and "God will be everything to everyone" (cf. 1 Corinthians 15:24, 28).
—**Pope John Paul II,** *Mission of the Redeemer,* 20

What one important truth did you learn from the above material?

_____

_____

_____

_____

_____

▶Closing Prayer Together

Pray the following prayer daily during the week prior to discussing this chapter; then close your discussion by praying it in unison:

You, LORD, have established your throne in the heavens, and your kingdom rules over all.

We extol you, our God and King, and bless your name for ever and ever. Every day we will bless you and praise your name for ever and ever.

Great are you, LORD, and greatly to be praised; your greatness is unsearchable. One generation shall laud your works to another, and shall declare your mighty acts.

On the glorious splendor of your majesty, and on your wondrous works, we will meditate.

All your works shall give thanks to you, O LORD, and all your saints shall bless you! They shall speak of the glory of your kingdom, and tell of your power to make known to the sons of men your mighty deeds and the glorious splendor of your kingdom.

Your kingdom is an everlasting kingdom, and your dominion endures throughout all generations. The LORD is faithful in all his words, and gracious in all his deeds. Our mouths will speak the praise of the LORD; let all flesh bless your holy name for ever and ever.

—Adapted from Psalms 103:19; 145:1-5, 10-13, 21

▶Notes

Chapter 5

Doing the Father's Will

Matthew 6:9-13

[9]Pray then like this:
Our Father who art in heaven,
Hallowed be thy name.
[10]Thy kingdom come,
Thy will be done,
  On earth as it is in heaven.
[11]Give us this day our daily bread;
[12]And forgive us our trespasses,
  As we forgive those who trespass against us;
[13]And lead us not into temptation,
  But deliver us from evil.

How to discern the will of God is a hot topic in books, seminars, and workshops, especially among young adults. Usually these teachings emphasize the practical aspects of discerning God's will by encouraging us to turn to Scripture, Church teachings, godly counsel, our circumstances, and prayerful listening to the Holy Spirit. All of these are helpful indicators, but, because of our humanness, no method for discerning God's will is foolproof. Often our subjective feelings skew how we read these signs.

As we learn about how to discern God's will, we could be tempted to believe that for some reason God is trying to hide his will from us. However, just the opposite is true. Two passages of Scripture are especially helpful in dispelling this misconception. John 14:21 says, "He who has my commandments and keeps them, he it is who loves me; and he who loves me will be loved by my Father, and I will love him and *manifest myself to him*" (emphasis added). This is a powerful promise that indicates that the Father and the Son desire to make themselves—and their will—known to us. Earlier in the Gospel of John (7:17), Jesus says that the key to knowing truth is the willingness to do his will. Or to put it another way, a predisposition to obeying God is a prerequisite to knowing what he wants us to do.

This brings us, then, to the gist of this third petition. The request is not "Thy will be *found*, on earth as it is in heaven" but rather "Thy will be *done*, on earth as it is in heaven." As Pope Benedict XVI pointed out in his book *Jesus of Nazareth*, "The essence of 'heaven' is that it is where God's will is unswervingly done. . . . The essence of heaven is oneness with God's will, the oneness of will and truth" (p. 147). This third request in the Our Father is concerned with fulfilling the will of God in our lives, our communities, society, and the world at large. Most of the Father's will is already revealed to us in sacred Scripture and Church teachings and through a pure and formed conscience that God makes available to each of us. We will have our hands full simply making ourselves familiar with and doing his readily revealed will!

We see in King Saul the human dilemma we all wrestle with in our spiritual formation—submitting our will to the Father's. Saul was chosen by God to be ruler of Israel after the people requested a king. Eventually Saul and the Israelite army were sent to defeat the Amalekites, and through the prophet Samuel, King Saul was told by the Lord how to deal with the spoils of victory. But Saul in his own wisdom laid aside God's instructions and decided to keep some of the spoils for later sacrifice to the Lord. God was upset with Saul's unwillingness to do what he had asked of him, as well as with Saul's audacity to think he had a better plan than God's. Through the prophet Samuel, God said, "Has the LORD as great delight in burnt offerings and sacrifices, / as in obeying the voice of the LORD? / Behold, to obey is better than sacrifice" (1 Samuel 15:22). The Our Father reminds us of this truth when we pray, "*Thy* will be done, on earth as it is in heaven" (emphasis added).

Again we must turn to Jesus to help us understand the depth of meaning that he intends through these words. The epitome of obedience, of doing God's will, is depicted in the Garden of Gethsemane, where Jesus prayed the night before his crucifixion: "Again, for the second time, he went away and prayed, 'My Father, if this cannot pass unless I drink it, *your will* be done'" (Matthew 26:42, emphasis added). This was obedience on earth "as it is in heaven." Doing the Father's will was the essence of Jesus' life and ministry, as the psalmist prophesied of the Messiah:

> Sacrifice and offering you do not desire;
>   but you have given me an open ear.
> Burnt offering and sin offering
>   you have not required.
> Then I said, "Behold, I come;
>   in the roll of the book it is written of me;
> I delight to do your will, O my God;
>   your law is within my heart." (Psalm 40:6-8)

This messianic psalm gives us two important insights about doing God's will. First, when we, like Jesus, set our hearts to do the Father's will, we will find delight in it and be fulfilled. Second, the key to obedience and delight is having an open ear to God and God's words within our hearts.

In this chapter, let's learn together what Jesus meant when he taught his disciples to pray, "Thy will be done, on earth as it is in heaven."

▶Learning from Scripture

1. In everything that pertains to life and godliness, Jesus is our model. Read John 4:31-38 and John 6:35-40, and describe the essence or core of Jesus' existence.

_____

_____

_____

_____

_____

_____

2   a. What important ingredient of doing the Father's will did Jesus demonstrate in John 5:19-22, 30?

_____

_____

_____

_____

_____

_____

b. How could we apply this lesson to our desire to do God's will?

_____

_____

_____

_____

_____

_____

3. Read Jesus' warning in Matthew 7:21, and then read the context (verses 13-23) of that warning. What is the chief evidence that we are entering the kingdom of God?

_____

_____

_____

_____

_____

_____

4. Jesus followed the warning in Matthew 7:21 with a helpful parable (7:24-29).
    a. What are the main differences between the two men in the parable? List two or three.

_____

_____

_____

_____

_____

_____

b. What does the foundation of rock represent?

_____

_____

_____

_____

_____

_____

c. What is the prerequisite for doing God's will?

_____

_____

_____

_____

_____

_____

5. Many passages of Scripture provide practical insights to help us live out our prayer, "Thy will be done, on earth as it is in heaven." Identify the main point of each of the following passages:
a. 1 Peter 4:1-2

_____

_____

_____

_____

_____

_____

b. Romans 12:1-2

_____

_____

_____

_____

_____

_____

c. 1 Peter 2:15

_____

_____

_____

_____

_____

_____

d. 1 Thessalonians 5:16-19

_____

_____

_____

_____

_____

_____

e. 1 John 2:17

_____

_____

_____

_____

_____

_____

6. Read Hebrews 10:14-17. How does God help us to do his will?

_____

_____

_____

_____

_____

_____

7. Identify one way the passages you have studied in this chapter can help you make progress in doing God's will.

_____

_____

_____

_____

_____

_____

▶Real-Life Lessons

Fr. Gereon Goldmann was a young Franciscan priest who as a seminarian was drafted into the German army during World War II. He was captured and held in an abbey as a prisoner of war and was then mistakenly interned in a French concentration camp in Africa as a Nazi war criminal. He served as priest for his fellow inmates while living in the most appalling circumstances. Yet there were prisoners serious about following Christ, and he used all of his spare moments to prepare sermons that he preached daily.

News of the havoc that was taking place in Germany would trickle into the concentration camp with an occasional letter. Fr. Goldmann describes the effect of one such letter:

> One man learned that a Russian tank had rolled over his wife and their four children. This was a man who had particularly loved his family, often showing around to the others the family portrait, his prized possession in camp. Now they were dead. He left his room and could not be found, and I feared we would find yet another suicide in a corner, as so often happened after one of these letters was received.
>
> I went to the chapel—and saw that the cross on the altar was missing. As my eyes grew accustomed to the darkness, I saw the missing man collapsed on the floor before the tabernacle, holding the crucifix in his hands. I tried to comfort him, but through his tears he stammered, "No, I need no word of comfort. Please help me pray what you preached yesterday."
>
> I thought back; it was a sermon on the Our Father, emphasizing the part that says, "Thy will be done." We prayed the Our Father together, and as he said the words "Thy will be done!" the battle was won. I felt the tension and the grief go out of him like a physical thing, so great was it, and he walked out of the chapel shining with strength and the will to continue. (Fr. Gereon Goldmann, *The Shadow of His Wings,* pp. 226–27)

▶Learning from the Church

In Christ, and through his human will, the will of the Father has been perfectly fulfilled once for all. Jesus said on entering into this world: "Lo, I have come to do your will, O God." Only Jesus can say: "I always do what is pleasing to him." In the prayer of his agony, he consents totally to this will: "not my will, but yours be done." For this reason Jesus "gave himself for our sins to deliver us from the present evil age, according to the will of our God and Father." "And by that will we have been sanctified through the offering of the body of Jesus Christ once for all."

"Although he was a Son, [Jesus] learned obedience through what he suffered." How much more reason have we sinful creatures to learn obedience—we who in him have become children of adoption. We ask our Father to unite our will to his Son's, in order to fulfill his will, his plan of salvation for the life of the world. We are radically incapable of this, but united with Jesus and with the power of his Holy Spirit, we can surrender our will to him and decide to choose what his Son has always chosen: to do what is pleasing to the Father. . . .

By prayer we can discern "what is the will of God" and obtain the endurance to do it. Jesus teaches us that one enters the kingdom of heaven not by speaking words, but by doing "the will of my Father in heaven."
—*Catechism of the Catholic Church,* 2824–2826

What one important truth did you learn from the above material?

_____

_____

_____

_____

_____

_____

▶Closing Prayer Together

Pray the following prayer daily during the week prior to discussing this chapter; then close your discussion by praying it in unison:

Father, your Son, our Savior, Jesus,
  found delight in doing your will.
All the heavenly angels and saints
  live to perform your will perfectly,
And in unity we pray, "Thy will be done
  on earth as it is in heaven."
Enable us to prepare for heaven
  by doing your will here and now.
Give us hope
  that we might find joy in doing your will.
Give us help
  that we might serve your will effectively.
Give us love
  that we might be properly motivated to do your will.
We ask in Jesus' name. Amen.

▶Notes

▶Notes

Chapter 6

Relying on God's Resources—
Grace for Today

Matthew 6:9-13

[9]Pray then like this:
Our Father who art in heaven,
Hallowed be thy name.
[10]Thy kingdom come.
Thy will be done,
    On earth as it is in heaven.
[11]Give us this day our daily bread;
[12]And forgive us our trespasses,
    As we forgive those who trespass against us;
[13]And lead us not into temptation,
    But deliver us from evil.

The first part of the Our Father directs our eyes and heart to God, enabling us to remember who we are praying to—our heavenly Father, the almighty powerful God, holy and worthy of all praise. This principle of focusing on God and having him clearly in mind is important. As we focus on this next petition, "Give us this day our daily bread," we can keep in mind that God is fully capable of answering this and all the subsequent petitions in our prayer. Focusing on God also helps us shape our petitions so that they are in keeping with his nature and will.

As we move from remembering and honoring God to asking the Lord for our needs, we need to keep another important principle in mind. When we pray, we should remember that we are one of many, not one alone. We are intimately connected to his body and therefore should offer our petitions on behalf of the family of God to which we belong. Notice the plural pronouns in the Our Father. Three times Jesus uses "our," and six times, the pronouns "we" and "us." Nowhere does he say "I," "me," "my," or "mine." This is not a selfish prayer, nor does it embody exclusive requests. This is an inclusive prayer; our individual needs are found and bound up within the common, universal needs of all of Jesus' followers.

Through this prayer, the Lord introduces his disciples to the idea of interdependent relationships, in which it is no longer every person for himself, but each for the other. That is probably why the request made by the mother of the sons of Zebedee to sit on Jesus' right and left hands (Matthew 20:20-23) seemed so crass and was such an affront to the other disciples. It was all about positioning *her* sons and was not in keeping with the prayer or the principles Jesus had taught them.

The request for bread appears on the surface to be about having our most basic needs met. Bread, in one form or another, is a staple of life. It is both appropriate and wise to ask for our daily sustenance from "Yahweh-Yireh," the God who provides. Isn't this really one of the values of saying grace, or thanks, over a meal? Shouldn't it remind us that even in good health and with a good job, God is the source of all that is good in life, even our ability to bring home the bread?

But we can also be confident that as Jesus referred to bread throughout his teachings, this petition took on a deeper meaning for the disciples. Review for a minute just a few of these powerful references to bread:

> Jesus took **bread,** and blessed, and broke it, and gave it to the disciples and said, "Take, eat; this is my body." (Matthew 26:26)

> One of those who sat at table with him . . . said to him, "Blessed is he who shall eat **bread** in the kingdom of God!" (Luke 14:15)

> Jesus said to them, "I am the **bread** of life; he who comes to me shall not hunger, and he who believes in me shall never thirst." (John 6:35)

> "I am the living **bread** which came down from heaven; if any one eats of this **bread,** he will live for ever; and the **bread** which I shall give for the life of the world is my flesh." (John 6:51)

Surely, our need for daily bread should remind us of our need for Jesus, the Bread of Life. Therefore, we should be willing to expend just as much effort to obtain and partake of Jesus, the heavenly bread, as we do our daily food. This petition should fill us with gratitude and make us aware that the world is full of people who are starving for their daily bread—and for the Bread of Life.

Let's delve more deeply into the ramifications of this petition.

▶Learning from Scripture

1. One of the most fascinating incidents in Israel's experience is God's provision of daily manna to feed the people while they were in the wilderness. Read this story in Exodus 16. What lessons do you see in God's provision?

    _____

    _____

    _____

    _____

    _____

2. Read Deuteronomy 8:3-18. How does God's provision of our daily needs form us in our faith?

    _____

    _____

    _____

    _____

    _____

3. The disciples lamented not having adequate bread to feed the thousands who came to hear Jesus. Read Mark 6:33-44 and 8:1-9.
    a. If you were a bystander and were privy to the conversation between Jesus and the disciples before he multiplied the food, what would have been your response?

    _____

    _____

    _____

    _____

_____
_____
_____
_____

b. What do these accounts teach us about trusting God to provide *our* daily food?

_____
_____
_____
_____
_____

c. What do they teach us about our involvement in helping meet the needs of those who are hungry?

_____
_____
_____
_____
_____

4.   Listed below are four other examples of God's provision of daily food. After thinking about each passage, explain how God diversely meets the daily needs of people.
     a. 1 Kings 17:8-24

_____
_____
_____

_____

_____

_____

_____

b. John 21:9-14

_____

_____

_____

_____

_____

c. Acts 4:32-37

_____

_____

_____

_____

_____

d. 2 Corinthians 8:12-15; 9:7-10

_____

_____

_____

_____

_____

_____

5. Where do you see yourself in depending on God for your daily bread? In being an instrument in his hands for answering the petition of others to "Give us this day our daily bread"?

_____

_____

_____

_____

_____

_____

▶Real-Life Lessons

Tom was in his first semester of college, seven years after graduating from high school as a marginal student—so he struggled. Attending on the G.I. Bill, he had little spending money, no savings, no car to travel into town, and no job. But because he believed that God wanted him to pursue his education, he had enrolled in college and trusted God to provide. Some would say he was presumptuous.

"One particular Saturday, I faced a lonely, and what looked to be a hungry, weekend," Tom recalls. "I was standing there looking at the dorm vending machine, trying to determine which items I could buy to get the most food for my last fifty cents. I was somewhat anxious, but I tried to face this predicament stoically and prayerfully."

Tom said he was in his dorm room studying (which was how he normally spent his weekends, trying to develop the study habits he had never learned in high school), when he heard a knock on his door. His good friends Bill and Ann had been on their way to visit another couple, when on the spur of the moment, they decided to drop in on Tom. They gave him two bags of groceries that they had bought for him on their way into town.

Some would say it was a coincidence. But Tom said that one way or another, God always provided. He thanked his friends and later thanked God for giving him his daily food.

▶Learning from the Church

When we pray, "Give us this day our daily bread," it may be understood that we are asking for our daily sustenance, that we have abundance, or at least that we may not want. . . . But if this prayer refers to our daily sustenance, then we should not be surprised if under the name "bread," other necessary things are also understood. . . . When we pray for daily bread, we ask for whatever is necessary for us on earth for our bodies' sake.

But Jesus says, "Seek ye first the kingdom of God and his righteousness, and all these things shall be added unto you." This is also what is meant by "Give us this day our daily bread." Our daily bread is the Eucharist, our daily food. It is good for us to receive that daily bread, which is necessary for this present time. When we pray this prayer, we pray for ourselves, that we may become good and may persevere in goodness and faith and a holy life. This is our wish, for if we do not persevere in this life, we will be separated from that Bread. Let us live so that we may not be separated from your altar, Lord.

Our "daily bread" is also the Word of God, which is laid open to us and in a manner broken day by day. And as our bodies hunger after real bread, so our souls hunger after this bread. And so our "daily bread" includes whatever we need in this life for both our bodies and souls.

—Adapted from St. Augustine, *Sermon 8 on the New Testament*

What one important truth did you learn from the above material?

_____

_____

_____

_____

_____

_____

_____

▶Closing Prayer Together

Pray the following prayer daily during the week prior to discussing this chapter; then close your discussion by praying it in unison:

Father, you are a God who provides, and you invite us to come to you for our daily bread.

We recognize that all that we have comes from your gracious hand, even our daily sustenance.

The bread of the kingdom of God is your Son, Jesus, who promised,

"I am the bread of life; he who comes to me shall not hunger, and he who believes in me shall never thirst."

We not only pray, "Lord, give us that bread," but also, "Thank you for giving us that very bread of life, Jesus' body and blood."

You give us daily bread that strengthens both body and soul.

Help us to distribute to the hungry bread that will nourish both body and soul.

In the name of the Father, and of the Son, and of the Holy Spirit. Amen.

▶Notes

▶Notes

Chapter 7

Relying on God's Resources—
Forgiveness and Forgiving

Matthew 6:9-13

[9]Pray then like this:
Our Father who art in heaven,
Hallowed be thy name.
[10]Thy kingdom come.
Thy will be done,
    On earth as it is in heaven.
[11]Give us this day our daily bread;
[12]And forgive us our trespasses,
    As we forgive those who trespass against us;
[13]And lead us not into temptation,
    But deliver us from evil.

The gospels indicate that Jesus was aware of what dwells in the hearts of men and women. St. Luke wrote that when Jesus was challenged by some in the crowds, he already knew their thoughts (11:17). St. John wrote that Jesus "knew what was in man" (2:25). This was undoubtedly true; Jesus knew that men and women are prone to sin and that we will have to continually come before our Father in repentance.

Jesus also knew that men and women are proud and that pride and insolence are the source of much conflict (see Proverbs 13:10). Inevitably, where there is conflict, there is offense and division that need forgiveness and healing.

It seems as if Jesus felt that the needs to forgive and to be forgiven were as basic as the need for daily sustenance, because when he taught his disciples to pray, he told them to ask their Father to "forgive us our trespasses, as we forgive those who trespass against us." In this prayer, Jesus forever linked our petition to be forgiven to our willingness to forgive others. We cannot be reconciled with God and be unreconciled with our brother, harboring anger or bitterness toward him. "For he who does not love his brother whom he has seen, cannot love God whom he has not seen" (1 John 4:20).

God has graciously given us the Sacrament of Reconciliation so that we can take responsibility for and confess our sins. In asking for absolution, we also need to have a spirit of forgiveness toward those who have hurt or offended us. When we do, the healing effect of this sacrament extends far beyond ourselves. It cleanses our spirit and the atmosphere in which we exist from the pollution of anger and malice. Conversely, when we fail to grant to others the kind of forgiveness we seek from God, a negative atmosphere sets in; and by it, many are hurt, including innocent bystanders.

Foundational to this petition is a spirit of humility. It is very humbling to acknowledge to God, or to a priest during reconciliation, the sins we have committed, especially when we confess very specific sinful behaviors or attitudes. Confession is contrary to our proud humanity. The natural response when we sin is to defensively shift the blame to someone or something so that we can assuage our guilt. Voluntary confession of our sins requires a supernatural response, which comes from the working of the Holy Spirit.

That is one reason why reconciliation with God and with people imparts grace to us: "Clothe yourselves, all of you, with humility toward one another, for 'God opposes the proud, but gives grace to the humble'" (1 Peter 5:5). Every act of forgiveness, whether we are requesting it or whether we are granting it to another, activates another infusion of God's grace. Conversely, we deprive ourselves of these graces when we know we should confess our sins and ask for forgiveness but don't do so, or when we withhold forgiveness from someone who has offended us. Through this petition—"forgive us our trespasses, as we forgive those who trespass against us"—Jesus introduces a spirit of mercy that enables our lives to constantly be infused with his grace.

As we review and discuss these passages on forgiveness, may we see them as they are—a glimpse into the very heart of the Father and of our Lord Jesus and central to the mystery of Jesus' death and resurrection. "Thus it is written, that the Christ should suffer and on the third day rise from the dead, and that repentance and forgiveness of sins should be preached in his name to all nations" (Luke 24:46-47).

▶Learning from Scripture

1. Matthew 18:21-35 provides a dire warning to those who fail to grant to others the forgiveness they seek.
    a. What precipitated Jesus' telling this parable?

    _____

    _____

    _____

    _____

    _____

    _____

    b. What attitude do you think may have caused Peter to ask, "How often shall my brother sin against me, and I forgive him?" (verse 21)?

    _____

    _____

    _____

    _____

    _____

    _____

    c. In what ways does the servant in this parable contradict the petition "Forgive us our trespasses, as we forgive those who trespass against us"?

    _____

    _____

    _____

    _____

    _____

d. Restate verse 35 in your own words.

_____

_____

_____

_____

_____

_____

2. Ephesians 4:31-32 says, "Let all bitterness and wrath and anger and clamor and slander be put away from you, with all malice, and be kind to one another, tenderhearted, forgiving one another, *as God* in Christ forgave you" (emphasis added).
    a. According to the following passages, what does it mean to forgive as God forgives?
    (1) Nehemiah 9:17

    _____

    _____

    _____

    _____

    _____

    _____

    _____

    (2) Psalm 103:10-12

    _____

    _____

    _____

    _____

    _____

    _____

(3) Isaiah 43:24-25

_____

_____

_____

_____

_____

(4) Luke 1:76-78

_____

_____

_____

_____

_____

(5) Luke 7:37-49

_____

_____

_____

_____

_____

(6) Luke 23:34

_____

_____

_____

_____

_____

_____

_____

_____

b. How would you define "forgiveness"?

_____

_____

_____

_____

_____

3.   Read 1 Peter 3:17-18; 2:20-24. How are you being Christlike when you offer forgiveness to someone who is unrepentant for having hurt you?

_____

_____

_____

_____

_____

4.   How do these passages change your attitude toward forgiveness or necessitate that you forgive someone against whom you are holding a grudge?

_____

_____

_____

_____

_____

▶Real-Life Lessons

Rick received the telephone call that every parent dreads: his son had been involved in an accident. Kevin wasn't driving; he had been walking home from his job at a local restaurant when he encountered a broken-down car. As he helped the driver push it off the road, a car driven by a young woman ran into him and killed him.

In the first few days after the accident, Rick vacillated between grief and a desire for revenge. As the court hearing on the accident approached, however, Rick was touched by the power of the Holy Spirit and realized that he *had* to forgive this driver, or he could not move forward with his life or in his relationship with Christ. So at the hearing, when the family members were given a chance to speak, Rick stood up and said to the young girl, "I forgive you."

The father of the young driver couldn't believe his ears. Several weeks later, he called and asked Rick how he was able to forgive his daughter. If the roles were reversed, the father said, he didn't think he could do the same. Rick explained that through prayer, God had given him the grace and strength to forgive her. Rick and the girl's father began meeting together.

Rick said, "Through our discussions and seeing what God has done in my life, the girl's father rededicated his life to Christ." Their relationship grew, and now as a team they freely tell their story at conferences and churches, so that people might understand God's forgiveness and learn about the power of forgiving one another.

▶Learning from the Church

With this petition, the Lord is telling us that guilt can be overcome only by forgiveness, not by retaliation. God is a God who forgives, because he loves his creatures; for forgiveness can only penetrate and become effective in one who is himself forgiving.

"Forgiveness" is a theme that pervades the entire Gospel. We meet it at the very beginning of the Sermon on the Mount in the new interpretation of the fifth commandment, when the Lord says to us: "So if you are offering your gift at the altar, and there remember that your brother has something against you, leave your gift there before the altar and go; first be reconciled to your brother, and then come and offer your gift" (Mt 5:23f.). You cannot come into God's presence unreconciled with your brother; anticipating him in the gesture of reconciliation, going out to meet him, is the prerequisite for true worship of God. In so doing, we should keep in mind that God himself—knowing that we human beings stood against him, unreconciled—stepped out of his divinity in order to come toward us, to reconcile us. We should recall that, before giving us the Eucharist, he knelt down before his disciples and washed their dirty feet, cleansing them with his humble love. . . . Whatever we have to forgive one another is trivial in comparison with the goodness of God, who forgives us. And ultimately we hear Jesus' petition from the Cross: "Father, forgive them, for they know not what they do" (Luke 23:34).

—**Pope Benedict XVI**, *Jesus of Nazareth*, pp. 157–58

What one important truth did you learn from the above material?

_____

_____

_____

_____

_____

▶Closing Prayer Together

Pray the following prayer daily during the week prior to discussing this chapter; then close your discussion by praying it in unison:

Have mercy on us, O God,
    according to your steadfast love;
    according to your abundant mercy,
        blot out our transgressions.

In experiencing your mercy,
    may we be merciful, as you are,
and as recipients of your love,
    extend your love through us.

Create in us a clean heart, O God,
    and put a new and right spirit within us,
a spirit of joy and generosity
    toward those who have offended us.

Restore to us the joy of your salvation,
    and uphold us with a willing spirit.
Then we will teach transgressors your ways,
    and sinners will return to you
as they discover your love and forgiveness in us,
    O merciful and gracious God. Amen.
—Adapted from Psalm 51

▶Notes

Chapter 8

Relying on God's Resources—
Protection from Evil

Matthew 6:9-13

[9]Pray then like this:
Our Father who art in heaven,
Hallowed be thy name.
[10]Thy kingdom come.
Thy will be done,
On earth as it is in heaven.
[11]Give us this day our daily bread;
[12]And forgive us our trespasses,
As we forgive those who trespass against us;
[13]And lead us not into temptation,
But deliver us from evil.

The last three petitions of the Our Father ask that a person be granted the means to sustain life, to enjoy a community of love and reconciliation, and to be free from the oppression of evil. Do these petitions reveal what Jesus thought were the essential concerns of life? If so, then praying this prayer puts our lives in perspective by helping us focus on what's really important, both for ourselves and for all the others who are included in that little word "us."

In addition, the Our Father, and the last petition in particular, help to dispel any doubts we may have that our prayers are not powerful or do not make a difference. Jesus taught his disciples to pray, because praying *does* make a difference.

The last petition also dispels any notion that the devil is not real. The devil who tempted the Lord in the wilderness was, and is, a real being. The Church describes him as a fallen angel (see *Catechism of the Catholic Church,* 391). Jesus knew Satan well and described him as "a murderer" who "has nothing to do with the truth," who has "no truth in him," and who "is a liar and the father of lies" (John 8:44). As Revelation 12 points out, he is the consummate deceiver and delights in accusing us to ourselves and before God, so that he can continually make war on us. He is not only a real being, he is a real problem from which we need a real deliverer.

And so Jesus taught his followers to pray, "Lead us not into temptation, but deliver us from evil." As the *Catechism* explains, "Our sins result from our consenting to temptation; we therefore ask our Father not to 'lead' us into temptation." Capturing the meaning of the Greek verb with a single English word ("lead") is difficult: the phrase "means both 'do not allow us to enter into temptation' and 'do not let us yield to temptation'" (2846).

Our temptations can come from the evil one or from our own disordered desires. "Each person is tempted when he is lured and enticed by his own desire. Then desire when it has conceived gives birth to sin" (James 1:14-15). This last petition of the Lord's prayer recognizes that any of these temptations can lead us into sin if we do not walk in faith and in dependence on the goodness of God. Praying daily that God will "lead us not into temptation" makes us aware of the dangers we will encounter and alerts us to flee from them. "A prudent man sees danger and hides himself; / but the simple go on, and suffer for it" (Proverbs 27:12).

However, we must always remember that the Lord is with us, even in the midst of our temptations. St. Catherine of Siena was afflicted with especially difficult temptations and attacks of the enemy. Once, after the temptations had passed, she communed with the Lord and asked him, "Where were you when my heart was disturbed by all those temptations?" The Lord indicated that he was in her heart, which was difficult for St. Catherine to believe. She asked, "How can I possibly believe that You were in my heart, Lord, when it was full of ugly, filthy creatures?" God then asked her if those thoughts brought her "delight or displeasure." St. Catherine replied that they brought her "the greatest sorrow and displeasure." The Lord then gave her, and through her gave us as well, tremendous insight into the battle with evil:

> "Well, then," said the Lord, "who was it that made you feel this displeasure if not I, who was hidden at the center of your heart? If I had not been there they would have entered your heart and you would have felt pleasure in them, but my presence there caused them to displease you." (Anne B. Baldwin, *Catherine of Siena,* p. 30)

Whether our petition is to escape temptation or to escape the attacks of the evil one, we can be confident of two things: one, we are praying in accordance with the Father's will; and two, he will be there with us, for he promises,

"When you pass through the waters I will be with you;
    and through the rivers, they shall not overwhelm you;
when you walk through fire you shall not be burned,
    and the flame shall not consume you." (Isaiah 43:2)

▶Learning from Scripture

1. What insights does Jesus' encounter with the devil in Matthew
    4:1-11 provide into temptation, the tactics of Satan, and God's
    deliverance?

    _____

    _____

    _____

    _____

    _____

    _____

2. a. What does James 1:13-17 teach us about trials and temp-
    tation?

    _____

    _____

    _____

    _____

    _____

    _____

    b. What are the spiritual benefits of testing and trials?

    _____

    _____

    _____

    _____

_____

_____

_____

_____

c. Give an example of such a benefit in your own life or in the life of someone you know.

_____

_____

_____

_____

_____

3.   a. After reading 1 Corinthians 10:12-13, list at least three things we can be assured of regarding temptation.

_____

_____

_____

_____

_____

b. When has God provided a "way of escape" from temptation for you?

_____

_____

_____

_____

_____

4. Describe the many ways God helps us to overcome temptation, according to Hebrews 4:12-16.

    _____

    _____

    _____

    _____

    _____

    _____

5. Read Hebrews 2:14-18. When we are dealing with the guilt of battles lost or the fear of failing future battles, what should we keep in mind?

    _____

    _____

    _____

    _____

    _____

6. How can you apply Ephesians 6:10-18 to your life so that it will help you overcome temptation and be delivered from evil?

    _____

    _____

    _____

    _____

    _____

▶Real-Life Lessons

For twenty years, Mike battled his addictive behavior. Then he re-embraced his Catholic faith, attending Mass, participating in small-group Bible studies, and joining a weekly men's group. Yet he still struggled as his addictive behavior intensified.

Here is how Mike described his battle with addiction:

When I was living a life of chasing earthly desires and carnal passions (including the use of illegal drugs), I continually put myself in places and with people that led me down a dark path, where I had no strength, either physically or spiritually, to say no or to walk away.

Finally, at a time when he was feeling quite vulnerable, Mike was given the grace to acknowledge his problem and make a clean break with the past.

When I came to a point in my life where I fully surrendered to God's love for me, I gave up all pretenses that through my own will, I could beat a lifestyle of drugs and alcohol.

Now, when I pray the Lord's Prayer, I ask my Savior that he not test me, that he shield me from those places and persons and thoughts that would lead me astray. It is only through my utter weakness and brokenness that I am made strong, made whole. It is only through God's strength and protection that I am kept safe from harm, away from the evil one.

And so I pray, "Lead us not into temptation, my dear Lord. I am weak; you are strong. Please do not put me to the test. Please hold me close, keep me safe. Only in your arms do I find refuge. Only in your arms am I made strong."

Through God's answer to Mike's prayers—as well as those of his wife, family, and many others—he is now thriving in Christ. But as

Mike's prayer demonstrates, he does not trust in his own strength, but in the Father's promise to "lead us not into temptation, but deliver us from evil."

▶Learning from the Church

The Holy Spirit makes us discern between trials, which are necessary for the growth of the inner man, and temptation, which leads to sin and death. We must also discern between being tempted and consenting to temptation. Finally, discernment unmasks the lie of temptation, whose object appears to be good, a "delight to the eyes" and desirable, when in reality its fruit is death. . . .

Such a battle and such a victory become possible only through prayer. It is by his prayer that Jesus vanquishes the tempter, both at the outset of his public mission and in the ultimate struggle of his agony. In this petition to our heavenly Father, Christ unites us to his battle and his agony. He urges us to *vigilance* of the heart in communion with his own. Vigilance is "custody of the heart," and Jesus prayed for us to the Father: "Keep them in your name." The Holy Spirit constantly seeks to awaken us to keep watch. . . .

The last petition to our Father is also included in Jesus' prayer: "I am not asking you to take them out of the world, but I ask you to protect them from the evil one." It touches each of us personally, but it is always "we" who pray, in communion with the whole Church, for the deliverance of the whole human family. The Lord's Prayer continually opens us to the range of God's economy of salvation. Our interdependence in the drama of sin and death is turned into solidarity in the Body of Christ, the "communion of saints." . . .

Victory over the "prince of this world" was won once for all at the Hour when Jesus freely gave himself up to death to give us his life. This is the judgment of this world, and the prince of this world is "cast out."

—*Catechism of the Catholic Church,* 2847, 2849, 2850, 2853

What one important truth did you learn from the above material?

_____

_____

_____

_____

▶Closing Prayer Together

Pray the following prayer daily during the week prior to discussing this chapter; then close your discussion by praying it in unison:

> LORD, you are gracious and merciful,
>> slow to anger and abounding in steadfast love.
>
> LORD, you are good to all,
>> and your compassion is over all that you have made.
>
> Your kingdom is an everlasting kingdom,
>> and your dominion endures throughout all generations.
>
> You, LORD, are faithful in all your words
>> and gracious in all your deeds.
>
> LORD, you uphold all who are falling,
>> and raise up all who are bowed down.
>
> Our eyes and hearts look to you,
>> and you give us the help we need.
>
> You, LORD, are near to us who call upon you,
>> to all who call upon you in truth.
>
> LORD, you preserve all who love you;
>> you hear our cry, and save us.
>
> And so we cry, "Save us, LORD, from every temptation,
>> and deliver us from every evil."
>
> We pray in Jesus' name. Amen.
> **—Adapted from Psalm 145**

▶Notes

▶Notes

Sources and Acknowledgments

Anselm. *Proslogion. Liturgy of the Hours.* New York: Catholic Book
Publishing Company, 1975.

Augustine. *Sermon 8 on the New Testament.* www.newadvent.org/
fathers/160308.htm.

Baldwin, Anne B. *Catherine of Siena: A Biography.* Huntington, IN:
Our Sunday Visitor, 1987.

Benedict XVI. *Jesus of Nazareth.* New York: Doubleday, 2007.

Columban. *Liturgy of the Hours.* New York: Catholic Book Publishing
Company, 1975.

Cyprian. Treatise on the Lord's Prayer. *Liturgy of the Hours.* New York:
Catholic Book Publishing Company, 1975.

Cyril of Alexandria. Homily 72. *Ancient Christian Commentary on
Scripture,* vol. III. Edited by Arthur A. Just Jr. Downers Grove, IL:
InterVarsity Press, 2003.

Goldmann, Gereon, OFM. *The Shadow of His Wings.* San Francisco:
Ignatius Press, 2000.

Guardini, Romano. *The Art of Praying: The Principles and Methods of
Christian Prayer.* Manchester, NH: Sophia Institute Press, 1957,
1985.

John Paul II. *Redemptoris Missio* (Mission of the Redeemer). Encyclical
Letter on the Permanent Validity of the Church's Missionary
Mandate. 7 December 1990. www.vatican.va/holy_father/
john_paul_ii/encyclicals/.

Te Deum. The Catholic Source Book. Orlando, FL: Harcourt Religion
Publishers, 2000.

Tertullian. *Liturgy of the Hours.* New York: Catholic Book Publishing
Company, 1975.

About the Author

Rich Cleveland and his wife, Gail, have been involved in ministry since 1974. Rich has served in several leadership positions at Holy Apostles Parish in Colorado Springs, Colorado, including as director of the Small Christian Communities Ministry. He and his wife have three grown children.

Rich also is director of Emmaus Journey: A Ministry of Catholic Evangelization and Discipleship. Through this ministry, Rich and Gail have published several Scripture-based Catholic small-group studies. Additionally, Rich publishes *Reflecting on Sunday's Readings*, a small-group study based on each Sunday's Mass readings, which can be downloaded for free from the Emmaus Journey Web site at www.emmausjourney.org.

Rich has served as speaker and seminar leader at numerous national Christian conferences and conventions, including the Franciscan University of Steubenville's Men's Conference, the National Council of Catholic Evangelization, St. Paul's Institute of Evangelical Catholic Ministry, National Fellowship of Catholic Men, and FOCUS.

Also by Rich Cleveland

Learn from Scripture about prayer, conversion, and faith from these Bible studies. The workbook-type format can help individuals seeking to understand Scripture, spouses who want to grow together in their faith, or Bible study groups.

Each Bible study features:
- Solid Catholic understanding
- Questions for thought or discussion
- Important Scripture passages for each topic
- Plenty of room to write

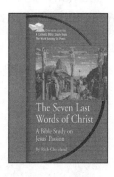

The Seven Last Words of Christ: A Bible Study on Jesus' Passion
The Seven Last Words of Christ will help you to meditate and pray with Jesus as he endured the agony of the cross. Learn to pray with Jesus, "Father, forgive them . . ." and hear his comforting words, "Today, you will be with me in Paradise."

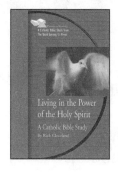

Living in the Power of the Holy Spirit: A Catholic Bible Study
Who is the Holy Spirit? What is his role in our salvation? How do we receive his fruits and exercise his gifts? These are a few of the questions explored in this nine-week Bible study, which is designed to help Catholics grow in their appreciation of the Holy Spirit and his power to transform their lives in Christ.

Stop by and see us as you journey on the Web:

Emmaus Journey: A Ministry of Catholic Evangelization and Discipleship provides Scripture-based resources and foundational training for small groups in Catholic spirituality

On the Emmaus Journey Web page, small-group studies are *free* to download and reproduce for use in your parish. You will find additional small-group resources and free downloads to assist you in your small-group ministry.

In addition, at The Word Among Us Web page, we offer *free of charge*
• the Scripture readings used at Mass for each day
• daily meditations and reflections based on the Mass readings
• practical articles on Christian living
• reviews of the newest Emmaus Journey Bible studies

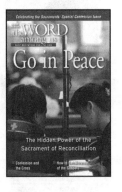

Please visit our Web sites today!

Emmaus Journey
www.emmausjourney.org
email: info@emmausjourney.org
phone: 719-599-0448

the WORD among us
www.wordamongus.org
email: theresa@wau.org
phone: 800-775-9673